Affiliate Marketing Step By Step Guide

Learn How to Launch an Affiliate Marketing Business So You Can Create Passive Income and Earn You Financial Freedom

By Adam Torbert

Table of Contents

Thank you for purchasing this book and I hope that you will enjoy it and find it useful. If you will want to share your thoughts on this book, you can do so by leaving a review on the Amazon page. It helps me out a lot.

If you are intereste in more book on similar topics about making money, then you may be interested in some of my other book:

Passive Income Ideas: Methods to Build Financial Freedom and Demolish Financial Stress

Dropshipping 2018: Guide to Making Money Online and Building Passive Income Through eCommerce in 2018 and Beyond

Digital Marketing Essentials: Learn About Digital Marketing And How To Use It To Leverage Technology To Get More Traffic, Boost Your Website Ranking And Build A Brand (SEO, Social Media Marketing...)

Day Trading for Beginners: A Complete Beginner's Guide to Setting up Systems and Strategies for Money Management and Earning Profits With Day Trading Opportunities (With Tips and Tricks...)

Introduction:

affiliate marketing is a standout amongst the most prevalent ways individuals profit on the web. It is where an individual partners up with a business so as to make a cut for himself by attracting guests to a business' specific item or business. In any case, It doesn't get simpler than that. To be extremely fruitful at profiting with subsidiary advertising there is somewhat more to it.

In the example of blogging, a blogger will turn into a member of a chosen organization and profit from being an associate by putting a hyperlink or anything else inside a blog entry that will redirect the visitors to that item or a business.

How precisely does an affiliate turn a profit? By bringing more traffic to a business of which they are an affiliate The hyperlinks and connections of the items you are endeavoring to have sold contain your one of a kind client ID when you install the HTML code into your website that influences the advertisement to show up.

At the point when the client clicks that promotion/interface/picture and purchases the item, the organization will be alarmed that you were the affiliate that drove them to that buy. Thusly, you will get a commission from the organization for being capable of driving new clients to their site.

It is imperative to comprehend which parties are included in affiliate advertising and those are mentioned underneath:

Advertiser – This is the organization offering the item who needs to pay other individuals to help items to be sold while also advertising the companies business. Sponsors, for the most part, give connections and the hyperlinks for the organization that is doing the advertising.

Publisher – this is the individual or organization that consents to advertise the item or business to acquire a commission. These publishers can distribute this data through web journals, sites and social networks in order to profit.

Client – the client buys an item subsequent to seeing the advertisement. The client is taken from the publisher's site to the merchant's site and finishes the deal.

One of the fundamental reasons why most novice affiliate marketers surrender following 3 months is because they can't drive traffic to their partner site. It's a pain for many marketers, yet one that can be effectively settled in the event that you put the work in.

As an affiliate marketer, you turn into an autonomous advertiser of a picked item or a selection of items from a certain category, for the seller's benefit. Doing affiliate marketing implies having outright opportunity to construct your online presence. It's your autonomous approach when or how you play your role and how you get to your clients and how you design the entire process. Sounds great? I wager it does.

Affiliate marketing is clearly the most effortless online plan of action to begin earning good revenue on the web. It doesn't have a lot of costs and the earning potential is good. Then again, it additionally may happen to be extremely tough. Everything is up to you and execution depends on your assurance, approach and the methodology you pursue.

With everything taken into account, the entire business is tied in with gaining a sales cut of offers. Like all things everywhere, associate showcasing has its upsides and downsides. If you're considering how to begin with this business, you should be aware of and investigate openings and difficulties and at that point this business empowers you to have a smooth beginning. How about we jump into the list of pros and cons? We will start with the pros.

Let's face it. An expertly assembled item that originates from somebody who as of now has a high level of validity makes it generally simple to sell. This is the reason top Internet Marketers still advertise affiliate offers right up 'til today while additionally profiting with their very own items since it's generally pain-free income with insignificant exertion required.

It is cost friendly: – domain name costs around 100 $ and under 10$ every month for web hosting that is good such as HostGator.com or BlueHost.com to have your very own WordPress-fueled site.

Passive income is another pro. Affiliate advertising is an incredible wellspring of passive income. Plenty of affiliates use it as an optional income stream while as yet working at their normal 9 to 5, or whatever it might be.

Affiliate marketing is flexible: Simply put aside a couple of hours every week to support and develop your online presence after the initial work of setting everything up.

You don't need to create a product. One imperative advantage of affiliate marketing is that you are not required to make or deliver any items. It is the obligation of sellers to make the items. So you are just required to choose the items to sell, get the partner hyperlinks and begin promoting. You can concentrate on just selling the item as you don't have to do anything with the creation or conveyance of the items.

Scalability: As your insight increments, you can rapidly and effectively increase your potential for earning, at long last enabling you to carry on with the way of life you've generally longed for, for you and your friends and family.

While subsidiary promoting is absolutely simpler than endeavoring item creation together with the business channel and all the rest, it's no stroll in the recreation center either. The basic certainty is that you do need to proactively advertise your site, keep the content new and applicable, constantly provide value, and guarantee that your affiliate program has a profound relationship to the niche you are working with. It is still necessary to discuss the downsides:

It Will require patience and Time. There is no shortcut, you won't profit medium-term. Affiliate marketing isn't an easy money scam.

It requires and demands an honest Effort. You are growing a genuine business, not simply engaging with some hobby. For instance, you should apply sensible exertion to get the word out about your site. Also, the odds of individuals discovering your site aren't too high.

Competition needs to be considered: If it is simple to agree to accept an Affiliate Program, then that means that it is simple for everybody, along these lines there could be a whole lot of affiliates for a similar program over the world and the amount of rivalry could be high.

Learning Curve might not be for everyone. Promoting via structured Sales Funnel is what the affiliate's income depends on. For instance, you will need to remain up to date about the best organic SEO strategies. In order to actually get a decent ranking on Google organically. This can be very tedious at first.

Chapter 1: Selecting Your Niche

Affiliate sites are a path for anybody to pick a subject, begin composing content, and ideally ensure a stream of passive income. Sadly, picking a niche without enough earning potential could mean that you get no results for a lot of work.

Prior to stressing over picking a good niche, you ought to see how affiliate marketers actually profit. They center around promoting items from other businesses in order to earn a commision.

An affiliate contract is a point at which an organization or an individual consents to pay an affiliate for fruitful referrals. For instance, Amazon has a program where they pay you a level of the business you create utilizing their hyperlinks. Affiliate marketing can be found everywhere these days.

Motivating individuals to believe your proposals comes down to two components: trust and expertise. The trust is earned by suggesting just items and businesses you are certain are of quality. The expertise depends on you developing a wealth of good content sufficiently wide to make you a specialist inside a given field. This is what you could call your niche.

While picking a niche, think about your pastimes and your interests. You're well on the way to appreciate building a site in a niche you as of now appreciate, which is why your hobbies are a good starting point. For instance, I am fond of video games so building a website around those would be a good idea for me.

The extraordinary thing about utilizing a leisure activity for your niche is your current knowledge about the subject. This implies you'll invest less energy into researching, which makes the composition procedure less distressing. Believe me, on the off chance that you pick a niche that you detest in some way or another, the work will be very unenjoyable. I discovered that when I attempted to compose many articles about cats. Never again.

On the off chance that picking something that interest you sound like the correct methodology for you, we should go over a couple of straightforward considerations to kick you off.

Make a rundown of your interests. Take some real time to contemplate to answer this. Which would you most appreciate sharing your thoughts about?

The next step is to find affiliate programs based on your hobbies and see which one has the most potential for earning.

The next step is to find affiliate programs based on your hobbies and see which one has the most potential for earning money.

Once you have compiled the final list of your past times that have the potential for affiliate marketing, you should research the market and see if the hard work is worth it based on the interest.

Once you have compiled the final list of your past times that have the potential for affiliate marketing, you should research the market and see if the hard work is worth it based on the interest.

Areas with low competition are what you should focus on. Niches vary based on how much people are interested in them.

The more interesting your niche is to people, the tougher it will be to infiltrate that niche. You will never have your own corner if there is too much competition. A quick google search should be all you need to see how many websites are there and based on that you can evaluate a niche. You should identify some specificity that would allow you to differentiate yourself. It is possible to carve out your sub-niche if you write for an unknown segment at the moment and that way you will easily achieve success if it happens to blow up and if that is your interest then you will have fun at the worst case and at the best case, you will have a business.

What you should focus on is spotting niches with low competition and enough traffic to make it worth the hard work. Compile a list of good potential niches and find out which are the most valuable keywords. Input those keywords into Google Keyword Planner so that you find out the search volume tor those keywords that you selected. Look at the results and focus on keywords that are searched for 3000 to 5000 per month.

You are attempting to design your website around several keywords that you determine are valuable. Expanding your audience is the ideal way to get more traffic. When choosing a niche you should focus on ones that give you an opportunity to go deep and to be profound. Targetting a niche with low competition is not a winning option. The smarter move to focus on areas a topic that allows you to deeply analyze them and this will always give you ideas and topics you could write about.

If you want to target more keywords, you should simply put your head down and produce more good content. You can expect this to be much harder if you are in a popular niche, but the potential reward is much greater.

Make a rundown of niches that allow you to analyze the, deeply such as cooking and keep searching and analyzing your choices until you come across a niche you can easily write about. The best scenario is finding a niche that you enjoy spending your time in and for which you are capable of writing deeply. You have hit a jackpot if you find something that is aligned with your hobby since you already enjoy doing it.

Don't forget that you won't be making money as soon as next week with affiliate marketing sites. You first need to have a whole lot of content before you can hope to see income that is worth writing home about. The more competition there is in your niche, the tougher it will be during your first weeks and months in your niche, so you have to keep your head up, have optimism and not give up. Good things happen to those who keep going.

What is also important is selecting a niche for your affiliate site and that will greatly affect the quality of your content. Your posts will never reach its intended group of people if you haven't properly selected your niche and all your hard work will be for naught. If you perform everything properly, then you may just have an interesting success story to tell as long as you are not afraid of hard work. To recap, in order to choose your niche, you have to look at your hobbies and interests in order to find ideas and topics and when you successfully figure out those ideas, then you have to find out it they can be monetized successfully. You will rank faster if you focus on areas that aren't too competitive. When you locate a niche that allows you to write deeply, then you will be able to write a lot and you are unlikely to run out of ideas soon.

In order to get started, you can read about the niches with the most money in them which can allow you to get directions and to not be completely lost. Such niches are listed and described below. The niches aren't listed in any particular order and all of them are great niches to sink your teeth in. Know which area you have the most expertise in and also what interests you the most so that you could make your decision as best as you could. You can't go wrong with the niches below if you want to be successful.

Beauty niche. The beauty list is always going to be near the top of the list when discussing the niches with a lot of money in them. All the products from anti-aging creams to hair products are included here.

Health and fitness niche. Everyone is looking for ways to get their health on a new level so that they could enjoy life more. Some of the reasons why people are interested in health are living longer or just enjoying lives without health problems. If you place your business around the health niche and the healthy living, it's hard to not to make money.

The survival niche. A lot of people can't wait to escape outside since a lot of us are stuck living the urban lifestyle for a good portion of our lives which disconnects us from nature. This niche focuses on unwinding and reconnecting with nature. For reasons listed, people will always be interested in activities like camping or fishing and for that reason, outdoor survival might be one of the best niches if making money via affiliate marketing is what you are into. Products will always sell under the conditions of high interest.

Luxury activities niche. When you hear someone utter the phrase „profitable niches“, what is the first thing that comes to mind? You probably think immediately of products that can't be bought for cheaply. And that immediate association is the reason why expensive hobbies niche is a part of this list. These are activities that require pricey gear such as golf clubs or drones and managing to sell those will net you a pretty handsome commission.

Self-improvement niche. Not many things will fulfill people as much as the feeling of accomplishment via self-improvement. Education and skill acquisition are examples of this and this niche might be the most profitable on this whole list, especially in the times we live in. A lot of this niche is intertwined with the IT niche since people want to find out how to use gadgets and leverage technology in order to make their lives better.

Gadget niche. Mobile phone and the most popular gadgets always seem to go hand in hand. Even though trendy gadgets could be really popular and a good opportunity to make money, they could be gone and forgotten in a day and you never know how much interest it will have and hwo long it will maintain it. There is always some new innovation and some new fad to take the place of ones that were really popular at one time. Tech companies are always trying to think of new ways to design gadgetsf better and to create something that will improve the customer's lives.

Fashion niche. Fashion has an influence on all of us to some degree and no one is truly immune even if they may claim otherwise. Whatever you are wearing now, you were probably influenced by someone or something. The fashion industry will always be around and thriving and latest accessories and clothing items will alwas be trying to get our attention.

Pets niche. If you have ever been on Instagram or on social media in general, you are surely aware of how much people are fond of animals. You can't even get through a week without coming across a barrage of dog videos and cats and dogs and so on. The point, people really do love their pets, more than people probably. They treat them like they would a family member and they don't hold back when it comes down to shopping for them.

Chapter 2: Choosing an Affiliate Program

Regardless of how much money you make with affiliate marketing, whether it only serves as a side income or a main full-time income, you have to find the right programs to promote. Don't proceed with the next steps until this is handled.

There are a lot of choices here and it may seem overwhelming at first, however, all that you need is a little guidance in the right direction and with that choosing the proper affiliate program will seem like second nature.

It should be compatible with your niche. You probably realize this yourself, however, it is important to state it anyway since making a mistake with this can sabotage your business before it even started and it is only a matter of time before it would come crashing down. You have to find products that are related to your website and your purpose. You have to engage your creativity here. If your blog is about cars, you don-t have to limit yourself to only cars by themselves. You could also write about car events and holidays and anything for which you are certain that it would be useful to your audience and that is why you have to know your key customer well.

Whatever you advertise as an affiliate marketer, your target audience has to have a desire for it. Again, you have to understand who is your ideal customer and this you should know even before you start your blog. The customer profile is something you should create in order to make figuring out your ideal customer easier. Imagine in your mind very clearly a person whom you are trying to help by selling your products and services. If there are already people that are paying you money for whatever you are selling, then use them as a reference for figuring out the characteristics of your audience.

Once you have a good grasp of your audience, you have to do your homework and spend some time researching if you want to make the right choice about an affiliate program. Do not rush this step and really put time and effort into your decision since the right decision now will make the road ahead so much easier.

There are many ways to figure out what your target audience wants and one way you should use is to pose a question to your question to your customers via a survey, or an email or a blog post or any other medium you could think of that would be appropriate. In case you don-t have enough people buying from you in order to make an accurate estimate, you should take a look at your competition in order to see what is hot and what are people interested in purchasing. Use social media to your advantage to figure out the problem and pain points you are trying to take care of. Those problems are what should be addressed with your affiliate program and you should choose it accordingly.

One method you can use is to put yourself in your customer's shoes. If you sell a product that you love and that you believe and for which you want to be a part of more peoples lives, then this business will be so much easier for you. You should make an effort to try the product out yourself and that is even more important if you actually don't know much about a product since that is the only way you will be able to present it with confidence. Learn what you can about the product by studying it and using it so that you can address any concerns about the product. You don't necessarily have to be passionate about the product for this to work, but you do need knowledge and you don't want any customer knowing more about the product than you.

If there are opportunities for upselling, use them. For those who don't know about upselling, upselling is a practice offering several complementary products to the customer at the moment of purchase in the hope of making additional sales and additional commissions. Bonus point if some products or some discounts are available only at the time of purchase.

One example of upselling would be selling a videogame console and offering a videogame or controller as a special deal. If this works and the deal goes through, then you can count on receiving more handsome commissions.

You must be selling a quality product. The product has to be a good one. The product is not a good quality one if a return rate is high because that is a sign that a lot of people don't like the product. If you want to succeed long term in business, then you have to make sure that your customers are happy and one way to achieve this is by having a high-quality product that you sell. Selling a high-quality product will ensure you a good reputation, and once you gain a good reputation, then you are settled as far as success is concerned and making sales in the future will be much easier.

Don't ignore the high ticket product that cost more. Even though you may want to stay away from this product, I advise you to rethink this because you may be thinking that they are way too hard to promote and generally not worth the hard work. You have a choice, you can either try to sell lower ticket product and then try to sell a bunch of them in order to make it worthwhile or you can find a high ticket product that you really believe in and only have to sell a handful of them in order to make good money. Both approaches work, but the choice is ultimately yours.

Successful affiliate marketers sell a combination of higher and lower ticket products based on the occasion and also because all people and customers are different and it is necessary to be ready to adapt to their needs in order to succeed in business. Having more options in terms of products will present your business with more opportunities.

Some merchants will offer you a commission which you can earn if you ensure that business gets a returning customer. This isn't so easy, but you will be handsomely rewarded for this since businesses know that returning customers are their greatest asset.

The reputation of the vendor you are looking to partner with is important and you should take it into consideration before you go ahead and sign a contract.

Every vendor has to start somewhere with their business but for your needs, it is advisable to pick someone with experience under their belt since those people have a good reputation which implies that there will be quite a bit of traffic which is good for obvious reasons. In order to make the right choice, you will have to do your research beforehand. You don't want to completely ignore vendors that are new since they may actually offer good products and be a good business partner, they just haven't had enough time to prove themselves yet.

By being a member of an affiliate marketing network, you can more accurately asses which vendor will give you best conversion rates and which vendor will generally be the best option. You should wait before committing to a new vendor since they don't have a lot of metrics to share yet. Earning potential is important, however, if you want to truly succeed, then you want to go for the product that you are passionate about even if it may give you a little less commission. Customers can see from a mile if you don't care about your products and that can sink you pretty quickly. Loving the product is important to be successful and to endure when it gets tough, and it will, it always does.

It is a great bonus if a vendor offers good support and that one thing can be a differentiating line between good and a bad choice. You want to know that a vendor has your back in case of some issues occurring and that assurance will really give you a piece of mind. Size of the vendor will have an effect on the medium in which the support can be offered, but it's still safe to say that you can count on an email option.

The availability and the quality of marketing materials that you can use is something you should evaluate when making your choice since it will be a huge help if you can play around with landing pages since using them successfully can really boost your success. Be mindful of what each vendor offers and which tool will be available for you to use before making your choice.

Make sure that the tracking period of cookies is long enough since it is a fact that a lot of customers won't buy anything during their first interaction.

By this point, it is safe to say that you are pretty confident about which product you will use to dominate affiliate marketing business and with that in mind you can start considering the commission options.

Don't be automatically fooled into thinking that higher commissions are generally always better just because they provide you with a higher number. You have to consider more than one dimension. It is possible that a product that offers high commission really doesn't sell all that much which will make it harder to achieve some kind of flow, while products that have lower commission actually tend to sell quite a bit and in a pretty good volume.

The average rate of orders will be affected by how much products are being sold and keeping that in minds, a low commission product with a higher average rate will surely trump over a product with a higher commission rate and lower average rate even though those both products may be sold at exact same price. The product with a higher average rate will put more money in your pocket.

Chapter 3: Building a Website

Your first affiliate marketing website creation doesn't have to be hard and you don't need to be a programmer in order to do it. It can be overwhelming if you've never created an affiliate website before, I can relate to that, but it only seems hard until it's done.

Your mind is probably racing with questions right now. You might be asking yourself should you outsource this whole website creation process and save yourself the trouble. You are also probably agonizing over which of many website builders will you use, maybe Wix, maybe Weebly or how about Wordpress or Squarespace? Do you have to be a certified programmer? These are just a couple of questions many people face when they are in a similar situation and it's nothing to be ashamed of.

It doesn't have to be hard, and if you continue reading, I will make it easy for you and you will be laughing when you remember that you may have been worried about it all. All that is required is that you follow the simple steps that are outlined in the continuation of this chapter and if you just do that, you could have your affiliate website live sooner than you think.

You are probably asking yourself how much you will have to pay for all this. You don't have to do the described process right away if you are currently strapped for cash, however, if you want to make money it is necessary to spend some money and there is a bit an upfront investment involved in building your website for affiliate marketing. Two things you will have to spend money on, and there's no way around this, is on a domain name and on a web hosting. Maybe those two terms are foreign to you at this moment but don't worry, you will have an understanding that you need as long as you continue going through this chapter. It is recommended to choose a service on a higher end of the quality spectrum since the website is an important part and a basis of your business and in order to get started, you can expect to be paying around 3$ a month.

If you are new to the website design then it is best to go with WordPress for designing your site and in case you are not really familiar with what WordPress is, it is essentially the largest and the most popular website builder in the world and you can use if completely free of any charge. It is begging to be utilized. However, you still need to be using previously mentioned website hosting and a domain name.

You need to get a domain name and a domain name is pretty much the URL of your website. Every website needs a name, however, in order to obtain a right to use a certain name for your website, you need to go through a domain register which is rather simple to do and is nothing to be overwhelmed by.

As far a web hosting is concerned, you need that in order to even have some visibility and perceivably on the web. There are numerous web services that can enable to have your web hosting which is equivalent to renting a web server for a price. Your website will never be discovered by the right people unless you are in possession of a web server. There is no need to get overwhelmed by this since there are numerous services that will take care of that entirely for you

In order to be successful at affiliate marketing, you can not be without these 2 services. There are free options available, but I strongly advise against using those for your actual affiliate marketing website from which you will be conducting your actual business. You can use free options to get some practice in, but definitely not for the real thing. It can be a bit of puzzle choosing a great domain name, especially if you are new to this whole affiliate marketing business. By this point, you already probably have chosen the niche around which your website will be based, so you already likely have a clear picture of what your website will be about. When looking for a domain name, you have to make sure that it is actually available. There is a bit of challenge here, but it is worth it for a good domain name since an attractive and great domain name is crucial for your website. You want to make sure that you choose the name you will be able to stick with and from which you will not deviate since changing a domain name in the future can lead to quite a few complications. Now I will discuss some factors you should consider when thinking about which domain name you will go with.

Do not use anything except .com. There are plenty of newer extensions that were invented and that are available, some of them being .net, .info and so on and new ones are appearing regularly, but still nothing has managed to dethrone .com as the main choice and that is likely to stay the same for a while. People do not like to change a good thing that is working well unless there is a good reason for that.

If you look at some successful business, they most likely use .com extensions and for the most part, most of the sites that you use on a daily basis will use .com extension as their primary choice since it still the big dog and will stay as such for a while. If you look at successful businesses and organizations and companies, it is quite unlikely that they are using .net or something like that. When you are new, just stick to what works and what is getting the results and do not try to change to conventions and to challenge the status quo just yet. Still, the impact of the extension is pretty small in the end and it is not something that you should overthink since it is not something which will determine if you will succeed or not, since it mostly depends on your content and your business savvy, so all that you should do is just go with the .com and move on to the next step since.

Next, do not use dashes for your domain name. Having only a single dash is unlikely going to be a dealbreaker in the end as far as your website climbing up in the search ranking is concerned, but things can get ugly if you introduce more than one dash since that can mess up the search engine optimization among the other things. It is hard to have an awesome domain name which also contains a dash. Such a domain can be decent, of course, but it will likely not reach the heights of greatness. It has also been determined that your trustworthiness will go down if dashes are included in a domain name. It takes less than a second for visitors to form their opinion about a certain website, and for many other things, for that matter, so you should ensure yourself against risk and just stick with a proven and tested formula of not using dashes.

Many people have used dashes in their websites and they regret their choice and you can learn from their mistakes and that way get to the success much faster, by having the right knowledge. The point is, using dashes and extensions other than .com are not dealbreakers, but the potential for your success will always be limited by using those things.

Next thing to take into consideration when choosing a domain name is that your domain name should have relevance for your target audience and to your affiliate website. The name that you choose should be a good description of what your site is about and it should form an immediate and correct association in the minds of the readers. The effect will be stronger by utilizing the shorter names, but if possible, you should try to include a relevant keyword that describes your website and your purpose adequately.

What you should also keep in mind when choosing a domain name is to make sure that there is a potential for building a brand around that name and this is not so easy and it does require you to squeeze the creativity muscles, but you will be rewarded and the chances for the success of your website or your blog will be greatly increased. Google is one prime example of this. It is a word that is completely made up and that was just recently added to a dictionary. The name is brief and memorable, even though it may not make any statement about the core business at first. A lot of words that have a branding potential are completely made up, Nike being another example, and these kinds of words increase your chances of getting a domain name for yourself that is not already taken.

Some final tips for choosing a domain name would be to ensure that the name is pretty easy to type and this is pretty crucial for your success on the web. Apart from dashes, you also want to avoid using other symbols such as numbers or hyphens. When numbers are involved, people can easily get confused and therefore, not be sure if they should type the number with letters or with numerals. The easier it is for the customers, the better. Before you jump onto a certain domain name, you should do your research so that you can be certain that a specific domain name that you have in mind is not already taken since you do not want to risk a trademark or a copyright violation.

Now that you know how to pick a domain name, or if you already have picked your domain name, now it is time to choose the web hosting service you will be using. You do not need to know much about web hostings or to be a programmer to do this step successfully. What you should be aware of that there is an absolute abundance of web hosting services and that options that you can choose are in the thousands. Even though there may be many options, the difference between different choices really isn't anything noticeable and this isn't something you should overthink too much. The good side of there being so many of businesses that provide web hostings is that they got a lot cheaper and for that reason, now is the best time to get started with a website.

What you want to look for when choosing a hosting service is that it is user-friendly and easy to use in general and this is even more important if you are not all that tech savvy at the moment. You should also make sure that whatever you choose, it can be integrated with WordPress and that a quality customer service is the part of the deal. Do not forget to pay attention to price. Wherever you look, there is no doubt that you will be presented with a wealth of different plans and payment options, but if you are just starting, then there is no reason to choose anything other than the basic plan just so that you could get started. You can upgrade to a higher tier when you are bringing in some money and after you have a proof of your concept working and bringing you success.

I will be using BlueHost.com as the example in order to explain how have your domain name registered and how to set up your web hosting along with installing WordPress. First, go to BlueHost.com and choose your plan for web hosting. Again, you want to stick with the essential basic plan for now until you are confident that you need an advanced plan in order to take your business to the next level. You can choose to upgrade your web hosting at any time when you think such a thing will be necessary.

By now you should have your domain name figured out, but even if you do not have it at this moment, you can choose to skip that step and to come back to it later once you have decided on the domain name. If you already have decided what your domain name will be, just enter it in the required box and move one.

Next, you will be required to enter all the details regarding your account and you have probably done similarly many times already, so just fill out everything that is required and move on.

Now that you have filled out everything, it is time to check your emails for a welcoming email which will provide you with a hyperlink that will enable you to choose your password. Set your password and make sure to remember it and not to use the same password for multiple services, especially in today's times. I personally keep all my passwords for everything in a word document and a simple ctrl+f command allows me to quickly find any password I need.

Anyway, now that you took care of your password, you will now be able to log into BlueHost by using that same password. You are just a couple of steps from your affiliate marketing website being live and available for business with anyone interested. You want to get acquainted with the dashboard so that navigating through it becomes natural.

The next step is installing WordPress. Luckily for everyone, installing WordPress is made very simple thanks to the consideration of BlueHost. There are a lot of free templates that you can use for WordPress and you are bound to find something that you fancy. These templates are already finished and built sites which you can pick as a basis for your site and you can design it to your own liking further on. Choose a template that you like, but try not to overthink this step too much, as so many people do. Picking a template is not a point of no return since you can revert the choice at any time. Install the theme after you have picked it.

Now you will be faced with a choice between business or personal use for your site. Since you are building this site with the intention of it being your affiliate site, you will be choosing a Business option. Now you will be facing a dashboard in Wordpress and you do want to get familiar with it. Once you are ready to really get started and to get down to business, you can do so by clicking the launch button. After that, you will be required to input your website title and its description. The title will be what people see as a result when they are on Google or any other search engine, for that matter, while the description will be what people will be able to read under the aforementioned title, so it is not hard to see why this requires attention.

And with that your first WordPress website is live and running. Now you can see it wasn't so bad. Any other small details you will learn about along the way as you continue simply using WordPress after which you will naturally get better.

Chapter 4: Creating Content for Affiliate Marketing

In order to be successful in affiliate marketing, you should be focusing on producing a sequence of content on a consistent basis over a period of time. If you manage to do that, writing quality and engaging content over a period of months, you will inevitably gain traffic, you just have to keep at it and think like you are one yard away from striking gold. This chapter is focused around giving you pointers for making the best content you can.

Do not create an affiliate marketing website in a way where it will be blatantly obvious that you are attempting to sell something, you do not want your affiliate website to come across as merely an online brochure. This is a mistake that a lot of beginner affiliate marketers make because they are putting money first without realizing that it is necessary to provide value first before asking for anything in return. You have to provide value first in order to get anywhere and you will do so by filling your website up with quality content and that is what this chapter is all about.

You are obviously doing this business to make money, but in order to do it successfully, you need to monetize the final part of the process after the value has been provided. After reading through this chapter, you can be assured that you will not be making a mistake when it comes to this.

What you have to do is to create quality content and this will attract the right kind of traffic to your affiliate website and this when you can start the selling process by offering a lot of great knowledge and after doing that for some time, they won't mind when you recommend purchasing a certain product or a service.

Your content has to be created around honesty. No one will want to purchase products in the long run if an affiliate marketer is promoting them just to make some money at the moment even though he or she does not really believe in the product or stand behind it. It may seem like something marketers do all the time, embellishing the product and making it look perfect under the spotlights while the real product may be average and not outstanding. Doing this can only work in the short run, but never in the long run, especially in the social media age where stories about bad business practices tend to spread really quick. Those are the kinds of stories that tend to go viral. In conclusion, you should at all times be honest about the products you are showcasing on your website. It will get really old if every product that you are introducing to the people seems like the best thing since sliced bread and people will see through that.

You are a marketer, but you do not want to make it obvious or to draw attention to that fact. You should utilize stories so that when you do mention a product, then the mentioning of that product will come across more as a recommendation instead of an outright sales pitch. If you can tell a story about your product where you attempt to vividly illustrate how it fits into what your brand is about, then your chances of success go way up. People love stories and they tend to learn better and memorize more that way and presenting content in that way will go a long way as far as building trust goes and trust is what will make selling that much easier, almost too easy.

It is recommended to show to your visitors in some way that you have actually used the product and the positive impact that was created by the utilization of the product.

Giving stories about your experiences and how certain products helped you is all well and good, but you should also remember that customers should come first and that you should focus on what customers love since you will make it way easier for yourself since you are aware of the demand and what people actually want. The fact is that what you like and what your readers like won't always overlap and that is unavoidable and it is necessary to be prepared for that. So when that misalignment does happen, you should shift your focus more towards what your readers actually want since that will ultimately determine your success.

You should always know in the back of your mind what do your customers actually want so that you could provide value at a moments notice, this goes back to doing your research and actually knowing and understanding your target audience. That knowledge is what will ensure your success.

You should attempt to keep things fresh and to add some variety to the way you do things since you don't want to come to the point where you become formulaic and stale. Variety is the spice of life. You should be able to recognize when it is time to introduce some variation into your strategy. This way you will make sure not to become mundane and unflexible blogger no one wants to read after a while and after the honeymoon period and by being adaptable you are also increasing your chances for attracting entirely new audiences and those new audiences can allow you a bit more versatility based on what they want and desire. In conclusion, you have to keep centered around what your readers like to see and also try to utilize more platform so that you can increase your presence further. All these tactics are utilized for the sake of keeping freshness and uniqueness alive.

Your content should give an impression to the reader that it is about them and it should give them a feeling of belonging and inclusion and relevancy and this is one thing that should not change and that should be the cornerstone of your website. If you want to be successful as far as affiliate marketing content creation is concerned, make it about readers so that they feel like it is about them.

You should understand your readers and their wants and needs and how far are they willing to go in order to achieve those wants and needs. You should be the person who makes fulfilling their wants and needs easier and you should be good at articulating what they have to gain by interacting with your business and the products you are promoting.

By doing as many of these things as you can, you will be creating valuable content and you will show that you actually give a damn about readers and that you can empathize and understand them.

One rule that you have to abide by is to not write or promote or be affiliated with the products that you haven't tried and never will and which you don't like or believe in. You are better off promoting a single product truthfully instead of promoting 5 products dishonestly.

Your readers have trust in you and they believe that you have their best interest in mind when talking about or recommending a certain product. Be careful with trust since it can take a lifetime to build and a moment to be broken.

Taking everything into consideration, you don't want to have products on your website with which you haven't had anything to do or which you secretly don't care about since people can see through that. All it takes is a handful of people to see through that and there lies the danger of losing credibility. Be careful, you don't want to have a bad reputation on the internet.

When presenting a certain product, you want to focus on specifically telling your readers and followers what is so great about it and why they should check it out and it is really hard to talk this way about a product you don't really care about and doing this more detailed approach successfully is what can really help your credibility and trustworthiness.

At this point you are probably thinking to yourself: „Yeah, yeah, I get it, focus on the people." However, you still want to keep search engines in mind and write for them too since they are getting smarter day after day and therefore, you should also consider how will search engines rank your website based on the content that you churn out. The safe way to do this is by knowing which terms and phrases and keywords that people are actually typing into the search bar when trying to find your website and then using those phrases in your content in a way that will seem natural and spontaneous. This is simple, but you can count on increased traffic as long as you implement this regularly and strategically. This is a form of SEO which stands for Search Engine Optimization and it basically refers to tweaking elements of your website so that your website would be treated more favorably by search engines, more on that in the next chapter.

Now that you know what you should keep in mind when you are creating content for your websites, here is the list of some forms of contents that are regularly created and you need to recognize what kind of content will be best suited for your website so that you could increase your chances of success.

Reviews. It is hard to run an affiliate marketing website without creating some reviews in order to promote and showcase certain affiliate products. This is all about writing about your experience and your thoughts about some product related to your niche and you could also be discussing why you use the product and in which way it benefits you Again, this has to be based on honesty. In order to not come across as a mere promotion, you want to be thorough and detail oriented so that people feel that they have gained something by consuming the content.

Product comparisons. This is somewhat similar to reviews, but the focus is on addressing some of the most pressing questions and concerns which people are bound to have. As mentioned earlier, you should view yourself as a customer and therefore you should already be aware of the common objections and worries and you should also know what your target audience values the most when making a purchasing decision. By comparing two products, you are using your understanding of the target customer in order to determine what is the best choice for them. By doing this correctly, a lot of questions will be answered and readers should have all the necessary information in order to make an informed choice.

How To articles. There is quite a bit of versatility as far as how to articles are concerned. Some general forms of how to articles can exist with the purpose of influencing the readers which course of action to take and what to buy, while other articles can focus on teaching and educating about how certain product is used properly.

Educational webinars. This form is often used by businesses with the purposes of product promotion and you, as an affiliate marketer, should be striving to do the same. Know what information is important concerning your affiliate products and create an educational webinar to cover that information. If your website is centered around listening to audiobooks and you are promoting some audiobooks as well, then you could create a piece of content such as: „10 tips to listen to more audiobook this summer." And by doing this your affiliate products are put into focus and attention is shifted onto them.

Keep in mind that educational webinars require more work to get produced than the other types, so you need to make sure that they are of a quality so that the payoff would be worth it in the end. It should be more dense with valuable information than your average piece of content. Webinars enable you to achieve a greater level of interaction and connection with the readers, so try to plan out beforehand how you will get people more involved and active. One example would be answering questions.

Gift Guides. This is a seasonal form of content and you will get the most out of it if you put out a gift guide around the holiday season since that is the time of the year when everyone is doing shopping like there is no tomorrow trying to get their loved ones gifts. Gift guides accompanied with affiliate links can be done at any time, but doing so during the holidays will guarantee the best results.

Seasonal content. Topics that people seek out during the year will change and vary based on what time of the year it is. For example, when Halloween rolls around, everyone is interested in costumes and it is a good time of the year to own stocks from companies that manufacture those costumes. Be aware of the seasonal trends that are related with your niche beforehand and make sure to be ready for them since sometimes it can take months of preparation before the actual season in order to truly reap the rewards. You want to be intentional about seasonal content up to the point of scheduling that content.

Longform guides. Businesses also love o use this tactic and this tactic is pretty good as far as collecting leads is concerned. The strength of this content type is in the fact that they are dense with quality information as opposed to shorter content variants and that is something that the reader will inevitably appreciate especially considering that it is done for free. This content for that reason has a better chance to be revisited or shared.

Video tutorials. For affiliate marketing, the text is the main format, but the fact of the matter is that a lot of people actually prefer to take in content in the form of video instead of actually reading it. This kind of content is a variant of how-to articles and it essentially educates the readers on how to use the product effectively that is being promoted. It helps if the products you are promoting via affiliate marketing aren't all that simple to use and has some complexity such as software. For a lot of people, video can prove to be a medium that can give them better presentation instead of words even though the same meaning is being conveyed and this is especially important with things such as website builders which do have some complexity to them. Watching someone use the product properly can assure viewers that they can do it too. One trick that you can use is to combine text and video and to use the video explaining the uses of a certain product and stick that video into a post that is conveying the same exact information.

Remember to keep putting your readers first by dealing only with products that you have personally used and which have left a positive impression on you for which you would like more people to have. If there are flaws, you should be honest about them and not sweep them under the rug. You should also remember to have a variety of approaches and that you should make use of stories since people learn the best that way. If you are regular with writing content for your affiliate marketing business and you have a strategy around it, then you can be sure that you will have success in the short run and in the long run.

Chapter 5: Search Engine Optimization for Affiliate Marketing

Search traffic is what will by large have an effect on if you will be making money with affiliate marketing. Increasing your traffic organically is one certain way of making more money in this business, no need to make things any more complicated. How many products you promote is what has a direct impact on how much cash you will be making from affiliate marketing. You should know your audience and promote your products based on what they want

First, you have to have to bring more people to your site by using search engines if you want to be successful in making sales. Your focus should be around organic traffic since such people from the search engine are more converting visitors since those people are already in the buying phase of the buying process and therefore it is easier to convince them and to sell to them. That is why you should learn how to boost your search traffic.

The main way you can increase your traffic is by focusing on keyword research and finding the proper keywords. If you are good at keyword research, then you can ensure that you will be getting a lot of traffic. Do not be one of the people who just write about what they want to write about without doing any keyword research beforehand, but you also don't want to deal with highly competitive keywords early on since you will find it very difficult to rank that way.

In order to do SEO properly and to really make money, you need to understand the main types of keywords. There are keywords that are based on information and there are also keywords that are based around actually having an intent of buying something. An example if keywords based on information would be typing something like "What is digital marketing", while keyword based around buying intent would be "Best digital marketing course" and in the latter, there exists an intent of actually going through with the purchase. In order to be successful, you need to know how to combine both of these types of keywords. People that are typing in keywords that are based on information don't have any intention of buying anything yet and therefore it is not advisable to make advances on such people. On the other hand, people that are typing in keywords based around buying intent have already made a decision that they are going to purchase something and to those people, it will be easier to sell directly.

Keywords based on information should be used to educate your audience about the products you are promoting. For that reason, it is necessary to clearly define your audience and to be aware of them so that you could have an idea of products you would like to promote to them and which products would be most suited for the occasion. Finding the right keywords for your website becomes a lot easier once you have this knowledge. Using the right keywords is what will increase your search engine traffic. More search traffic is what will bring in more sales. You should be making attempts to find the keywords based on the information so that you could educate more people about your products and about what you are offering.

You also need to make attempt to discover the most ideal keywords that are based around buying intent since these are the keywords that ultimately lead to sales. You can't go wrong with writing a lot of reviews about products since that way you will draw in people that are searching the reviews of various products. This way you are accomplishing two goals, you are providing the necessary knowledge to your visitors and you are also earning money by selling your affiliate products via the affiliate links which you are using strategically.

When you are writing product reviews, make attempts to write without bias and don't try to misrepresent the product to make it seem like something other than what it is just in order to make a couple of extra sales. You should also be mentioning some of the negatives of the products since this way you will come across as more trustworthy. When you earn the trust of your audience, then you can be sure that you will be making some sales. You should also have used the product yourself before you actually go selling it. Don't write a review about something which you have never had any experience with. After using the product, you will have an idea whether you are satisfied or not and only then can you write a review. Audience and readers will be more likely to buy if they actually see some results of the products being used.

As mentioned before, you should be using a combination of keywords based on the information and the keywords based on buying intent since people don't purchase on the web from someone they don't know and for that reason, you cant be using only the keywords that are based around buying intent. You have to put the initial effort of educating your audience and giving them an idea of what you are about and making them comfortable. That is where your affiliate marketing website comes in since you will be using it to provide your audience online with a greater understanding of your products and that is where keywords based on information comes in.

Keywords based on buying intent are the ones which you want to be using when you recognize an opportunity based on the activity on the blog. The combination of these types of keywords is something you should know how to gauge based on your experience and doing so will improve your ranking on search engines over time which will lead you to more sales.

In the previous chapter, types of content that you could be making were listed, however, in the following part, you will be able to find out which kind of content will contribute most towards your sales. If you want to make money with your affiliate marketing website, you need to get your content marketing down. As long as you are creating the right kind of content, you can make sure that you will be seeing more sales.

The first form of content you should be focusing on are video tutorials since creating videos about the products you are promoting is a pretty certain way of increasing your sales and in these videos, the focus is on showing how certain products are used. Do not forget to include an affiliate link somewhere nearby. Video content can allow you to achieve pretty good conversion rates and it is a pretty good form for everyone, from beginners to experts.

Ebooks are something you should also be putting out since people like reading eBooks and you should be using them to solve customer's problems and you should also be using them as an opportunity to include your affiliate links. As long as Ebooks are good and as long as they are providing sufficient value, you can count on them to influence a lot of readers to follow the affiliate links and to take action on making a purchase.

You should also be using case studies in which you will be giving a detailed overview of a product. This content should cover all that is necessary to know about a certain product and it should do it well so that the audience wouldn't have to go elsewhere to get any additional information. This is possibly the toughest form of content to create and it does require most effort, but it will pay off and it will be worth the effort as long as it is done well.

Affiliate product comparisons can work well when it comes to ensuring that you get more affiliate sales. The point of this is comparing two products that are actually quite similar instead of comparing products that are complete opposites and by doing that you are able to really talk about characteristics of the product and to show how much you actually know. At the end of this demonstration, you should give a clear and unambiguous conclusion so that the readers would without a doubt know what to buy and which action to take.

One type of content that you can't do without and which pretty much every affiliate marketer depends are reviews of products. Just take a look at any successful affiliate marketers website and you are likely and you will see that that person often writes product reviews. The simple reason for doing this is the fact that reviews work pretty well. Product reviews provide readers with a better understanding of what you are offering and the reviews are actually quite convenient and inoffensive manner of providing affiliate links. Reviews simply work, but only if they are honest and without the biases so that the audience could make an informed decision that would ultimately benefit them.

Next, there are certain resources which you should be using in order to make sure that your SEO is as good as it could be. If you use the following tools and resources properly, you are bound to see improvements with your affiliate marketing business. Definitely, don't sleep on these tools if you want to be successful.

Google Keyword Planner is a widely recognized and used tool that is also free and marketers from all around use them to discover keywords and search terms. All that is required in order to use Keyword planner is to have a Google Adwords account and you can start finding keywords just like the best of them.

SEMrush is yet another tool you should be using and it is the tool which will help you keep track of your competition. SEMrush will help you realize which of the keywords are bringing in the most results to your competition and it will also aid you in realizing which are the ideal products to be selling to your audience.

Long tail keywords are what you should be using in order to get more search traffic. Longtail keywords are longer keywords and they are more specific than the short tail keywords. For example, "affiliate marketing" is a short tail keyword, while affiliate marketing for absolute beginners" would be a long tail keyword and these long tail keywords are easier to rank for. Long Tail Pro is one tool that makes discovering these long tail keywords pretty easy. This tool can find the best keywords for any market.

MOZ keeps being touted as one of the best SEO tools that are actually used by experts. Moz can actually show you how your website is doing and it can give you recommendations and pointers about what you can actually do as far as improvements are concerned. MOZ can even tell you how you can improve each page via its page optimization feature and it does it in a very user-friendly way such as telling you which keywords to use or which image would be most appropriate.

Ubersuggest is the tool which can be used to research keywords and to also figure out the intent that is behind those keywords. Ubersuggest will help you with using the appropriate keywords for your website and it will provide you with suggestions. It gets even better, this tool is free and there is nothing from stopping you from using it.

Google Trends has been around for a while, but it still isn't utilized by many people as much as it should and you would be wise not to make that same mistake. Google Trends can give you a background on each keyword and it can also inform you about trends regarding a certain topic or a niche.

Next, in order to improve the SEO of your affiliate website, you should be analyzing the competitive content and this will help you with on-page SEO. In order to do this, you have to top websites and blog for the keywords you are interested in targeting and you should analyze and see how they are designed around certain keywords. You should be analyzing if they have keywords in important places such as the title, subheading, URL, meta descriptions, sales copy etc. By doing an analysis of this kind you can get an understanding of what may be lacking and what you could do in order to position yourself for these keywords. SEMrush is an invaluable tool to accomplish this.

Just like analyzing your competitors, you should also analyze your own website and your posts. Use Google Analytics in order to find out which blog posts are providing you with the most traffic and also try to find out to what point are those posts optimized for some important keywords and why are they getting the success that they are getting. If you can successfully determine the reason for your success, then you can extract that and come up with a formula for repeating that success.

Know which SEO elements are the most essential and always remember to focus on those. Know which is your primary keyword and make sure to use that same keyword several times in your posts. Make sure to scan for and to recognize an opportunity to insert your main keyword into the content unsuspiciously. It is better to not use the keyword at all instead of using it in a weird and offputting way. That main keyword should also be used in your title. You can attach an alt tag to every image that you use and make sure to use the main keyword as those alt tags. Your main keyword should also be part of the URL.

To end this chapter on a helpful note, I will include some tips that will help you considerably on your journey to improving your SEO and getting your page out there.

Focus on building an email list. If you are looking for a guaranteed way to create trust between you and your audience, building an email list is that way. As long as your readers trust you and as long as you are delivering and adding value, you will be making sales week after week. There is a right way to do email marketing and the next chapter of this book is all about that.

Make sure not to start in a general and broad niche. That is a beginners trap and doing so won't work as far as becoming a successful affiliate marketer is concerned. You should be promoting highly targeted products in order to achieve lasting success. You will do better by offering fewer products that are targeted instead of offering more products that miss the mark.

You should start small and focus on improvement and learning and not to treat affiliate marketing like a get rich quick thing. Identify which skills you have to have to be successful and focus on improving those, money problem is usually a skill problem. You won't likely be making money during your first couple of months and that is why you need to have proper expectations and a long term perspective.

Chapter 6: Building an Email List For Affiliate Marketing

There is one thing which can provide you with more sales and traffic than Facebook, Instagram, Twitter or any other form of online advertising. What I am referring to are Email lists. Email lists can enable you to really connect with your audience and that is what will really increase your sales.

There are many reasons why Email marketing works so well and one of them is the fact that you can personalize your messages and you can send that directly to the inboxes of your potential customers. You have the permission to send emails as long as someone has joined your email list, but you should not abuse this and it is ideal when people are actually happy and curious when you send them an email. You want to be welcome in their inboxes. If someone has given you their email address, then that means that a certain person is already interested and that they already have a reasonable amount of trust in a product or a brand. Email marketing is what generates additional traffic and it also forms loyalty.

MailChimp is what you want to start with and what you want to get familiar with in order to make big bucks with email marketing. MailChimp is the platform which gives you an option of sending several thousands of emails at one time. You can also track and analyze your metrics and then vary your approach based on them. It is also surprisingly simple and just with a little practice, you can be sending email campaigns just like the best of them.

Signing up for MailChimp is completely free and it will remain free until you collect 2000 subscribers, although when you reach those numbers, upgrading to a higher quality package shouldn't be a problem. This is a really budget-friendly way of getting started. Now that you have signed up for MailChimp, it is time to create your first list. There are several options available from the start, but for now, in order to start building an audience, the only thing you should click on is to "Create a List" and this will be where all the email addresses will be kept and stored. By keeping track of your list, you will be able to identify who are your most valuable customers. You can, for example, see who opens your emails more than others. The list tells you how your customers behave and that way you can determine who your most valuable customers are.

Next step is creating a signup form and this part is pretty crucial. The signup form is a window that is placed onto your website and that window is what gives visitors an option of providing their contact details. MailChimp really makes creating these forms simple and it provides you with several options of doing so. In order to place a form onto a website, it is necessary to select an embedded form. MailChimp also gives you an option of designing and stylizing your signup form. When you are done, then you are provided with a piece of code which you will be using to put the signup form on your website, so make sure you keep it safe.

Next step is embedding your website. If your website is on WordPress, then you can simply download the MailChimp plugin which will give you a plethora of options to place your signup form on your website. On the off chance that you are hosting the website by yourself and not using WordPress, in that case, you can simply paste your code into the HTML file. That is all there is to it. Each and every time someone uses that form to sign up for an email list, the contact info will go directly into your list.

Now that your list is in its starting stages, it is necessary to learn how to send newsletters. In order to do so, select to start a new campaign from the main menu and even though there are several types, you are best off by sticking with the standard campaigns and that is the one which you should be using most of the time. Now you will also have an option of designing which you do by dragging and dropping and here you are limited only by your creativity although it is not necessary to go too crazy here and it is better to be practical and to stick with what works. There are numerous pre-made templates that you can choose. If there are any images that you want to use, then you simply upload it and the same applies to social media content and videos.

Every time before you send out a campaign, make sure to send a test first. It is good to have a separate email address just for receiving that test. Make sure to check out what the message looks like on a couple of different browsers and also on a couple of different devices, even though MailChimp allows you to preview what the email will look like.

When you are ready, send the campaign. After a campaign is sent, all that is left is checking the stats and MailChimp makes that really easy by making them real time and that means that you will start seeing the metrics as soon as a couple of hours after your emails are sent.

In order to get to the point of your career where you are sending out thousands of emails, it is necessary to have what is called a lead magnet. A lead magnet is an extra piece of value which you are offering to your audience in exchange for their email address. The content of the lead magnet can range from an Ebook to a piece of software. Whatever it is, it has to have enough value for your target audience so that they would make a decision to give away their email address and that is one more reason why it is necessary to know your audience.

You already subconsciously know what lead magnets are if you've been on the internet for some time and there's a good chance that you have signed up for a couple. Lead magnets are what will really get you a lot of email addresses. Again, this content has to be useful to your target audience. You can create the lead magnet yourself or you can outsource the creation.

Now that you have your lead magnet, it is still necessary to set it up on your site and to set up the system which will provide new members with links to their lead magnets. In order to do so, you will head over to the page where you will click to create a new sign up form and this time you will choose to create a general form. Now you will be creating a so-called "Thank You" page and this is essentially where your audience will be redirected after they have filled out the signup box. On this page, they should be able to clearly see the link which will lead them to a lead magnet after they click on it. After you set up this system, MailChimp will be doing the rest and the work of sending out thousands of emails.

The process of creating a lead magnet is as simple as that and as long as your lead magnet is on point, you will be collecting email addresses in no time! All that is required now is to send regular newsletters and over time, this is how you build loyalty among your followers. You will know you are doing it right if they are looking forward to an email from you. Just stick to the essentials and you will quickly be dealing with thousands of email addresses and sending them exclusive offers and deals is how you make the big bucks.

Conclusion

The main reason for loving affiliate marketing so much is because there is no need to deal with customers and to deal with complaints or with anything. All you have to do is to market the product. Find the product that you like and market it to the right people.

I also love all of the tools, there are so many useful tools that will help you with affiliate marketing business and they are completely free and just lying there begging to be used by ambitious people. There are so many different approaches and so many angles that you could take in order for you to make money with this business. There is so much you can do.

It is also about freedom and being able to spend time with people you want and to do the things that you want and to be able to travel and to be tied down by the clock for the best hours of the day. Digital marketing is all about leverage, you can set up systems and let them run in your sleep. That's why you should join digital marketing, leveraging technology can do so much for you and it is truly the best way to live. So if this is something you are interested in and something you want to achieve, then Take action as soon as you can, since motivation from this book is temporary and it wont last more than 24 hours.

I hope that you enjoyed this book and that it will help you in creating the passive income that we all want. If you would like to share the thoughts on the book, then you can do so by leaving a review on the Amazon page. Have a great rest of the day!

Printed in Great Britain
by Amazon

78430988R00041